OFFICERS & SOLDIERS

The FRENCH ARMY during the Great War

Volume I. 1900-1914

The Army in France

General Staff, Saint-Cyr, Infantry, Mountain Infantry, Chasseurs à Pied, Chasseurs Alpins, Cuirassiers, Dragoons, Chasseurs à Cheval, Hussars, Artillery, Engineers, Balloons, Military Aviation, Supply Train, Gendarmerie, Services, Quartermaster, Administration, Military Telegraphs, Treasury and Post, Medical, Veterinary

The Army of Africa

Zouaves, Algerian Tirailleurs, African Light Infantry, Foreign Legion, African Chasseurs, Spahis

Colonial Troops and the Navy

Colonial infantry, Senegalese and Malagasy Tirailleurs, Colonial Artillery, Sailors and Marines

André JOUINEAU

Translated from the French by Alan McKay

HISTOIRE & COLLECTIONS

The Infantry

Infantrymen on 2 August 1914 were not very different from their elder brothers of 1870, except for a few uniform details. The kepi changed its shape but not the colours it inherited from the Second Empire. An attempt was made to camouflage it since soldiers were provided with blue muffs to dull the red of the cap.

The famous *garance* (madder red) trousers were worn by nearly all the soldiers in the French Army, ever since the end of Charles X's reign, even though less conspicuous materials, like reseda, were tried out in 1911. This was thought to be too German and was not adopted and so madder red, "the symbol of France", endured. It was thought that some government deputies used these trousers as an excuse to protect the local production of natural madder, a plant used for dyeing, but there was nothing in this: this particular colour was obtained, and had been for a long time, from synthetic alizarine imported from Germany.

The main item of clothing in the campaign - the greatcoat - was worn in all circumstances, no matter what time of year. Wearing it, together with the heat wave during August 1914, considerably hindered the infantrymen who were already overloaded: each man carried *"his home on his back"*, i.e. his haversack containing all his campaigning impedimenta, to which were added tools and unit utensils, all this weighing some sixty pounds.

The only area in which there had been any real development over the last 35 years was in weaponry: the Chassepot rifle had been replaced by the 1886-93 8-mm Lebel repeater rifle, which greatly increased firepower and range. The appearance of the machine gun, a group rather than an individual weapon, played an important role in this development. But when Europe mobilised the strategists, though quite aware of the weapon's formidable potential, were nonetheless incapable of setting down how it could be used rationally. In August 1914, a regiment had six machine guns, shared out into two sections per battalion.

The NCOs were dressed like the rank and file except for the sergeant-major who had an infantry 1845-model sabre and a revolver instead of a rifle.

The officers, like the adjutants, wore a lighter but no less indiscreet uniform, the breeches with a black stripe being also madder red. The iron-grey smock replaced the black tunic. The officer's kepi was covered with a blue muff. He also carried a cape or a light coat which could be worn saltire-wise, or at best, the troop's greatcoat.

The Army of Africa landed in France in its traditional *"oriental"* uniform, which was hardly adapted to modern warfare. Zouaves and tirailleurs wore white *sarouals* (Arab trousers) with a jacket and waistcoat, dark blue and sky blue respectively. The equipment, except for a few details, and the weapons were common to all the infantry.

The Senegalese Tirailleurs were part of the Colonial Infantry. They fought and lived barefoot or wearing light sandals. The battalions which were brought to the front in France in autumn 1914 were given large-sized boots which got a mixed reception, and the onset of the cold season brought up the question of warm clothing. They were issued with the Chasseurs Alpins' dolman smocks and infantry greatcoats.

The Cavalry

At the beginning of the 20th century the French Cavalry's appearance was still something spectacular. But it too had ignored the proposals for reform intended to make the troopers less conspicuous when facing the formidable steps forward weapons had made in recent times. In 1914, the cuirassiers still looked like their elders at Reichshoffen (1870).

The steel helmet and the breastplate gleamed in the sun and a solution had to be found to remedy this. Shortly before the war a helmet cover made of light khaki cloth was issued but there were no plans to do away with the breastplates. A few attempts were made to camouflage them before mobilisation - they were anecdotal. During the first days of the campaign, the troopers were no longer obliged to polish their cuirasses, and they were even allowed to dirty them or put a sack or a padded waistcoat over them. But this did nothing to make the breeches any less conspicuous.

The dragoons dressed in dark blue but also wore madder red trousers, like everybody in the cavalry except for the spahis. They also inherited the lance, a weapon first issued during the First Empire to fight the Cossacks with. The lancers, the arm's sub-divi-

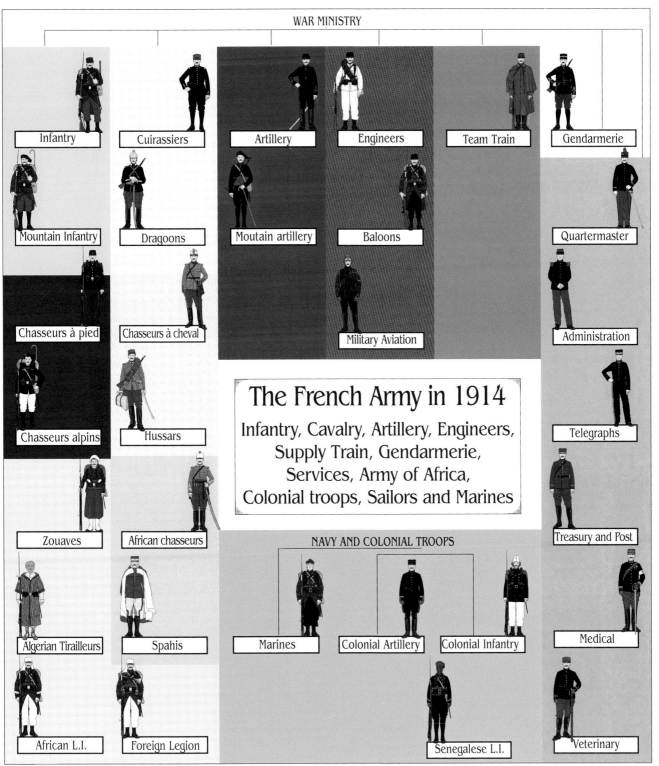

WAR MINISTRY

Infantry

Cuirassiers

Artillery

Engineers

Team Train

Gendarmerie

Mountain Infantry

Dragoons

Moutain artillery

Baloons

Quartermaster

Chasseurs à pied

Chasseurs à cheval

Military Aviation

Administration

Chasseurs alpins

Hussars

Telegraphs

The French Army in 1914

Infantry, Cavalry, Artillery, Engineers,
Supply Train, Gendarmerie,
Services, Army of Africa,
Colonial troops, Sailors and Marines

Zouaves

African chasseurs

Treasury and Post

NAVY AND COLONIAL TROOPS

Algerian Tirailleurs

Spahis

Marines

Colonial Artillery

Colonial Infantry

Medical

African L.I.

Foreign Legion

Senegalese L.I.

Veterinary

5

sion, had disappeared with the Second Empire and the lance was abandoned temporarily, then reintroduced in the dragoons and the light cavalry. This weapon whose iron point was mounted on either a bamboo or a steel tube was used alongside the 1822-model sabre with a slightly curved blade and an 1890-model cavalry carbine.

The light cavalry mentioned consisted of chasseurs and hussars wearing sky-blue, differentiated by their collars and facing tabs. They wore shakos.

In August 1914 a regiment of chasseurs, the 5th, wore the 1913-model helmet with a hunting horn on the band. Chasseurs and hussars were issued with the same equipment and weapons: 1822-82-model light cavalry sabre and 1890-model cavalry carbine; equipment was the same as for the dragoons.

The harness was standard for all the cavalry except for the spahis, and except a few equipment details and the colour of the blanket.

The Artillery and the Engineers

The Artillery had always worn dark blue and their uniform's visibility was therefore less problematic, even more so as the artillery did not fight in the front line.

In 1914, almost all the Artillery was horse-drawn. The 75-mm canon, its main weapon with 3 860 pieces in the order of battle, was drawn by a team of six horses, with three mounted drivers on the left-hand horses and three gunners who rode on the trunk-bench on the limber.

Within the context of the offensive doctrine, only a part of the heavy artillery was mobilised and the absence of heavy calibre pieces made itself felt even during the early weeks of the campaign.

The Engineers were dressed like the Artillery and could be distinguished by their velvet collar tabs with scarlet numbers. The arm gathered together several specialisations among which bridges, railways, signals, balloons. The latter however were abandoned as they could not be included in any offensive doctrine. They were therefore removed except over the strongholds.

In the first days of the campaign however the High Command became aware of how useful these balloons could be, brought them back into service and then set about improving their equipment together with that of the six winches. Apart from the balloons there were also airships.

France was a pioneer in this domain with Germany and possessed five, used principally for long-range reconnaissance and bombing.

The Military aviation

Created a few years earlier within the Engineers, in 1914 this new arm was still only used for reconnaissance and observation. There were 21 squadrons in the Military Aviation and three squadrons for the Cavalry.

These machines were among the most modern of the time.

There was however no set of guidelines put forward as to how they were to be used. Each pilot who took off on a clear day and did so to observe and reconnoiter for the army groups. It was thus that two pilots from the entrenched camp that Paris had become were able to observe von Kluck's manoeuvres, confirmed later by other observers, which enabled the September 1914 counter-offensive to be mounted.

Apart from personnel seconded to the aviation who wore their original arm's uniform, in 1914, Military Aviation personnel wore the Engineers' uniform with their specialisation's own particular insignia and the pilot's armband with wings.

The Navy

When the war started, the Navy had two coastal cruisers, 32 cruisers, 86 torpedo boats, 128 patrol boats, 34 submarines, 8 armed boats, 4 minelayers and 7 minesweepers. Apart from defence tasks in the Atlantic alongside the Royal Navy, its main job was in the Mediterranean protecting the shipping lanes between North Africa and Metropolitan France from attacks by the Austrian Navy.

From the autumn of 1914, the French Navy also took part in the land fighting with, on the one hand naval gunnery units serving the first high-powered long-range pieces set up on the front, and on the other a brigade of navy fusiliers commanded by Admiral Ronar'ch.

The latter, fighting in Flanders was assimilated into an infantry brigade.

The uniforms for both the sailors and their officers were particularly simple and rational.

The General Staff

Brigadier-general wearing full dress, on foot. The brigadier-generals wore a striped sky blue sash-belt whereas the major-generals wore red striped ones with two rows of oak leaves

Major-general wearing a dolman-smock

Brigadier wearing a coat

Major-general wearing a tunic. The breeches were embellished with a double black stripe separated by black piping

HQ staff hussar brevet-captain, on the staff of a cavalry division

HQ staff dragoon brevet-captain, on the staff of a cavalry division

7

Rank markings for Other Ranks

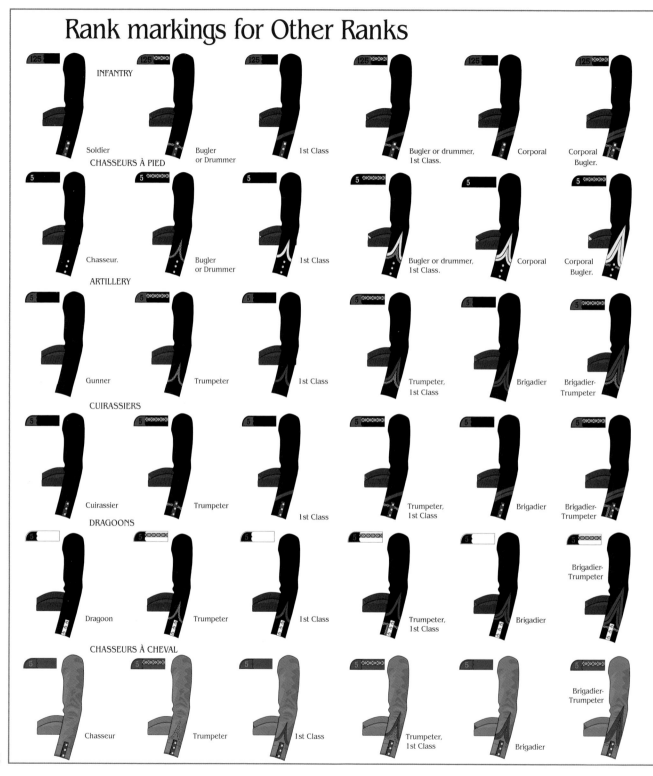

INFANTRY

Soldier — Bugler or Drummer — 1st Class — Bugler or drummer, 1st Class. — Corporal — Corporal Bugler.

CHASSEURS À PIED

Chasseur. — Bugler or Drummer — 1st Class — Bugler or drummer, 1st Class. — Corporal — Corporal Bugler.

ARTILLERY

Gunner — Trumpeter — 1st Class — Trumpeter, 1st Class — Brigadier — Brigadier-Trumpeter

CUIRASSIERS

Cuirassier — Trumpeter — 1st Class — Trumpeter, 1st Class — Brigadier — Brigadier-Trumpeter

DRAGOONS

Dragoon — Trumpeter — 1st Class — Trumpeter, 1st Class — Brigadier — Brigadier-Trumpeter

CHASSEURS À CHEVAL

Chasseur — Trumpeter — 1st Class — Trumpeter, 1st Class — Brigadier — Brigadier-Trumpeter

Rank markings for NCOs

INFANTRY

Re-enlisted Corporal-Farrier

Reenlisted Sergeant. They were allowed to wear the straight-collared tunic as going out dress

Sergeant-Major

Drum-master

Drum-major. In full dress he wore the adjutant's kepi with a tricolour plume

Adjutant

Adjutant-chef. This rank was created in 1913

LIGHT CAVALRY

Re-enlisted Brigadier-Farrier

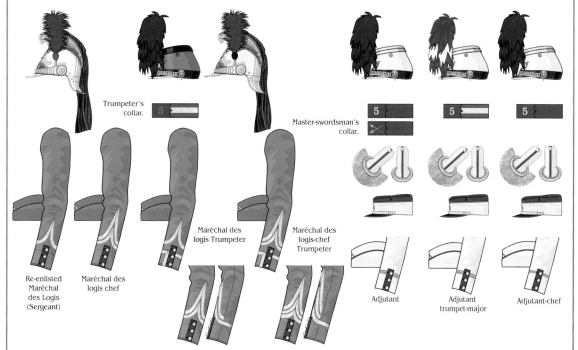

Trumpeter's collar.

Master-swordsman's collar.

Maréchal des logis Trumpeter

Maréchal des logis-chef Trumpeter

Re-enlisted Maréchal des Logis (Sergeant)

Maréchal des logis chef

Adjutant

Adjutant trumpet-major

Adjutant-chef

Special Military School

Exercise dress wearing an infantry greatcoat

Mobilisation dress, 2 August 1914

Mounted squadron full dress

Full dress parade uniform

Full dress shako plate, with button and collar tab

Mobilisation dress for the pupil when he was incorporated into an infantry regiment as a sous-lieutenant

Rank markings for officers

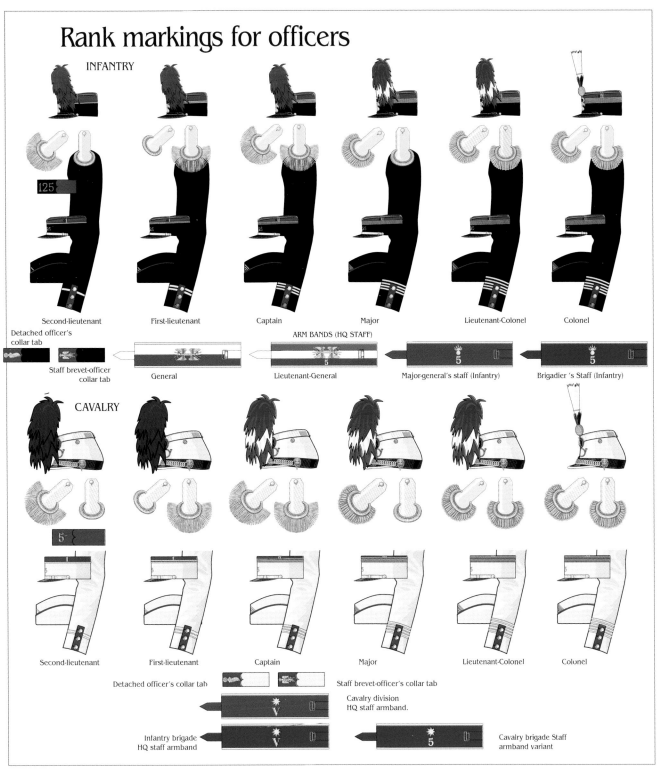

INFANTRY

Second-lieutenant

First-lieutenant

Captain

Major

Lieutenant-Colonel

Colonel

Detached officer's collar tab

Staff brevet-officer collar tab

ARM BANDS (HQ STAFF)

General

Lieutenant-General

Major-general's staff (Infantry)

Brigadier 's Staff (Infantry)

CAVALRY

Second-lieutenant

First-lieutenant

Captain

Major

Lieutenant-Colonel

Colonel

Detached officer's collar tab

Staff brevet-officer's collar tab

Cavalry division HQ staff armband.

Infantry brigade HQ staff armband

Cavalry brigade Staff armband variant

The Infantry

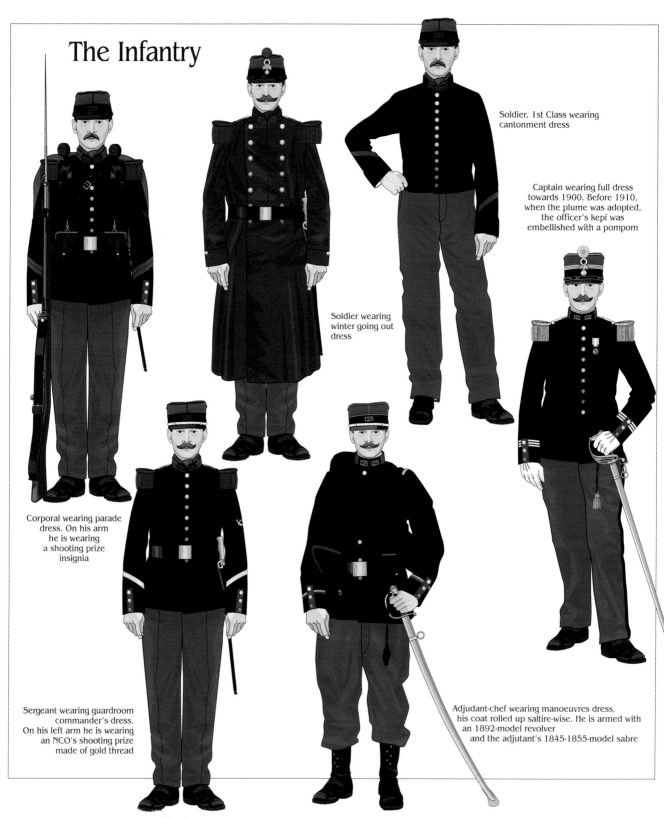

Soldier, 1st Class wearing cantonment dress

Captain wearing full dress towards 1900. Before 1910, when the plume was adopted, the officer's kepi was embellished with a pompom

Soldier wearing winter going out dress

Corporal wearing parade dress. On his arm he is wearing a shooting prize insignia

Sergeant wearing guardroom commander's dress. On his left arm he is wearing an NCO's shooting prize made of gold thread

Adjudant-chef wearing manoeuvres dress, his coat rolled up saltire-wise. He is armed with an 1892-model revolver and the adjutant's 1845-1855-model sabre

The Infantry

Soldier in fatigues dress with the 1882-model natural linen blouse and trousers

Corporal in summer manoeuvres dress

Soldier wearing cantonment dress

Cook in working clothes

Regimental (male) nurse

Soldier wearing summer cantonment dress. The forage cap was normally worn according to the regulations without any insignia which could however be a grenade as here, or the regimental number

13

The Infantry

Mobilisation dress. The 1884-model kepi was covered with a blue muff. The greatcoat was the 1877-model and the madder red trousers the 1867-model. Equipment consisted of an 1893-model haversack with suspender straps which held the 1888-model cartridge pouches. The belt is the 1845-model. The one-litre (two-pint) flask is the 1877-model, the bag the 1892-model and the boots the 1893 or 1912-models. The rifle is an 1886-93 Lebel

Captain wearing mobilisation uniform. He is wearing the 1913-model bluish iron grey smock. His madder red trousers are embellished with a black cloth stripe

Kepi number plate (hidden under the muff)

Sergeant-major wearing mobilisation dress. His armament was identical to that of the adjutants

Traffic-warden from a territorial unit armed with a Gras rifle and appropriate cartridge pouch

Collar tabs. From top to bottom: One-figure regiment. Three figure regiment. Reserve regiment (add 200 to the active number). Territorial regiment. Officer with embroidered numbers.

Regimental cyclist. Wearing the uniform and carrying the weapons of the cavalry, he was issued with a smock used by the Chasseurs Alpins with his speciality insignia on the collar. His armband bears the regimental number

14

The Mountain Infantry

The mountain infantry wore all the infantry of the Line's uniforms with a few modifications related to conditions of life in the mountains: alpine beret, white wool belt, calf bands

Corporal wearing parade uniform. He is wearing the 1889-model alpine beret. On the other hand the jacket and the rank markings were the same as for the infantry. The sash-belt was made of wool. The madder red trousers were tightened on the calves by leggings. Weapons and equipment were those of the infantry

Drummer Corporal

Soldier wearing cantonment uniform

Soldier, 1st Class wearing a greatcoat

Top to bottom:
Troops' collar tab
Officer's collar tab

159

158

The buttons are the infantry's

Corporal wearing natural linen blouse

Lieutenant wearing service dress. A gold ribbon-wire grenade has been sewn onto his beret

15

The Chasseurs à pied

Rank and file's mobilisation dress (here a corporal) and that for an officer. Except for the distinctive colours, the uniform was identical to that of the infantryman's

Tool carrying sapper wearing cantonment uniform. His speciality insignia, peculiar to the chasseurs – a spade crossed with an axe - was sewn onto both sleeves

Battalion commander wearing parade dress

HONNEUR ET PATRIE

ISLY
SIDI-BRAHIM
SEBASTOPOL
SOLFÉRINO

RÉPUBLIQUE FRANÇAISE CHASSEURS À PIED

Chasseurs à pied flag as it was when it was presented on 14 July 1880. In 1887, the inscription "EXTREME-ORIENT" was embroidered onto it,

"MADAGASCAR" was added in 1896, and then "MAROC" in 1914. Guarding the flag was entrusted by decree to the 10th or the 24th Battalions

Corporal wearing cantonment dress

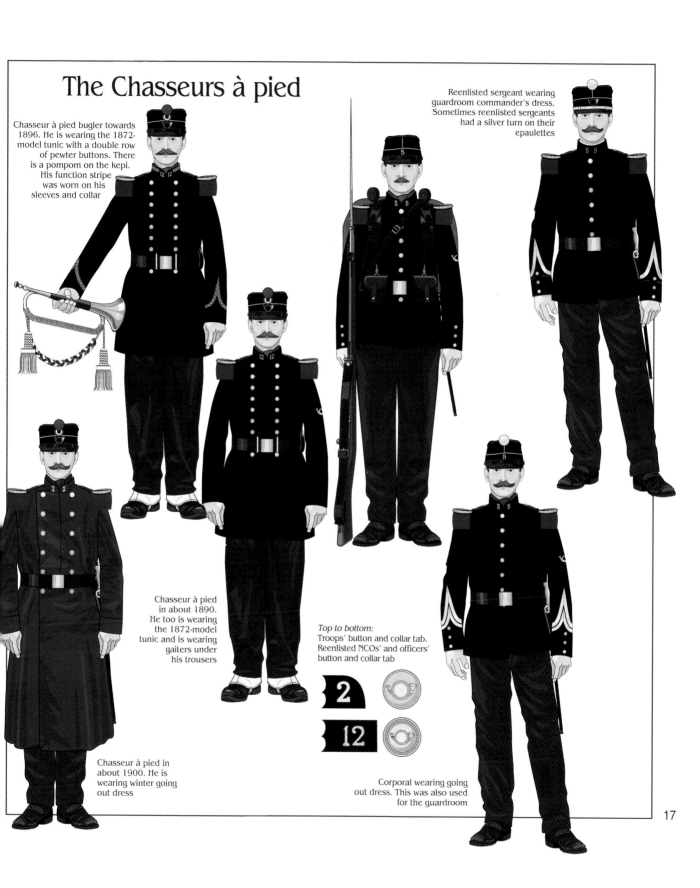

The Chasseurs à pied

Chasseur à pied bugler towards 1896. He is wearing the 1872-model tunic with a double row of pewter buttons. There is a pompom on the kepi. His function stripe was worn on his sleeves and collar

Reenlisted sergeant wearing guardroom commander's dress. Sometimes reenlisted sergeants had a silver turn on their epaulettes

Chasseur à pied in about 1890. He too is wearing the 1872-model tunic and is wearing gaiters under his trousers

Top to bottom:
Troops' button and collar tab. Reenlisted NCOs' and officers' button and collar tab

Chasseur à pied in about 1900. He is wearing winter going out dress

Corporal wearing going out dress. This was also used for the guardroom

17

The Mountain Battalions of the Chasseurs à pied

Chasseur
mule driver

Bugler, 1st Class wearing
summer dress

Chasseur wearing
summer dress

Sergeant-major wearing
going out dress. Under his
stripes is the silver and
scarlet reenlistment braid

Chasseur wearing
barracks dress with
a dark blue jersey

The Mountain Battalions of the Chasseurs à pied

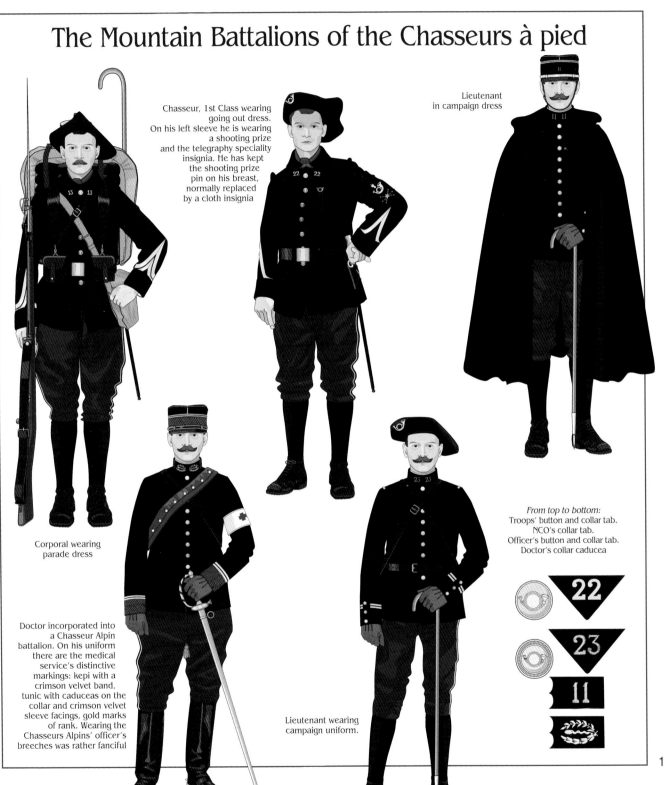

Chasseur, 1st Class wearing
going out dress.
On his left sleeve he is wearing
a shooting prize
and the telegraphy speciality
insignia. He has kept
the shooting prize
pin on his breast,
normally replaced
by a cloth insignia

Lieutenant
in campaign dress

Corporal wearing
parade dress

Doctor incorporated into
a Chasseur Alpin
battalion. On his uniform
there are the medical
service's distinctive
markings: kepi with a
crimson velvet band,
tunic with caduceas on the
collar and crimson velvet
sleeve facings, gold marks
of rank. Wearing the
Chasseurs Alpins' officer's
breeches was rather fanciful

Lieutenant wearing
campaign uniform.

From top to bottom:
Troops' button and collar tab.
NCO's collar tab.
Officer's button and collar tab.
Doctor's collar caducea

The Cuirassiers

Cuirassier wearing mobilisation dress. Unlike the other branches of the cavalry, the cuirassiers wore their sabre on the offside to leave space for the carbine, held in place in a sheath. In fact this weapon could not be carried slung over the shoulder because the man was wearing a breastplate

Officer's and soldier's buttons. The cuirassiers were the only sub-division of the cavalry to have an embossed button.

The Cuirassiers

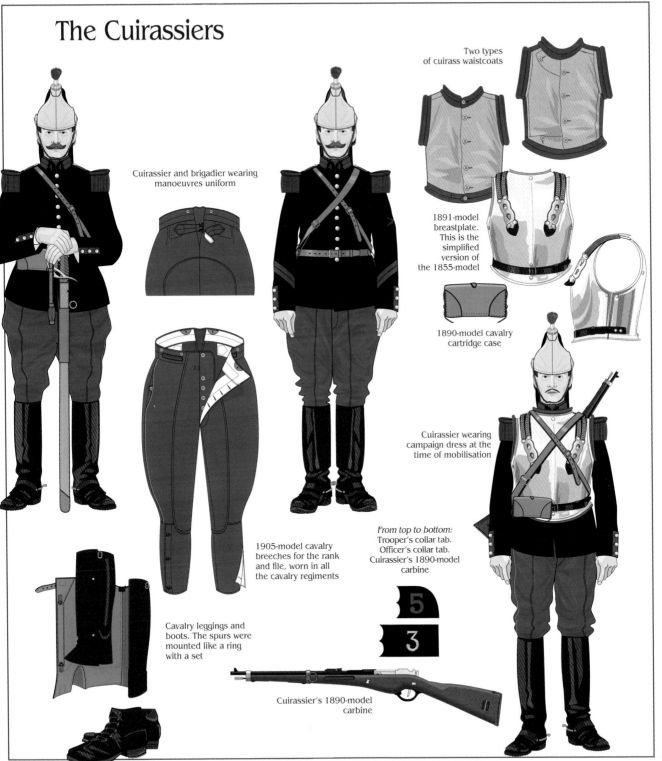

Cuirassier and brigadier wearing manoeuvres uniform

Two types of cuirass waistcoats

1891-model breastplate. This is the simplified version of the 1855-model

1890-model cavalry cartridge case

Cuirassier wearing campaign dress at the time of mobilisation

From top to bottom:
Trooper's collar tab.
Officer's collar tab.
Cuirassier's 1890-model carbine

1905-model cavalry breeches for the rank and file, worn in all the cavalry regiments

Cavalry leggings and boots. The spurs were mounted like a ring with a set

Cuirassier's 1890-model carbine

The Cuirassiers

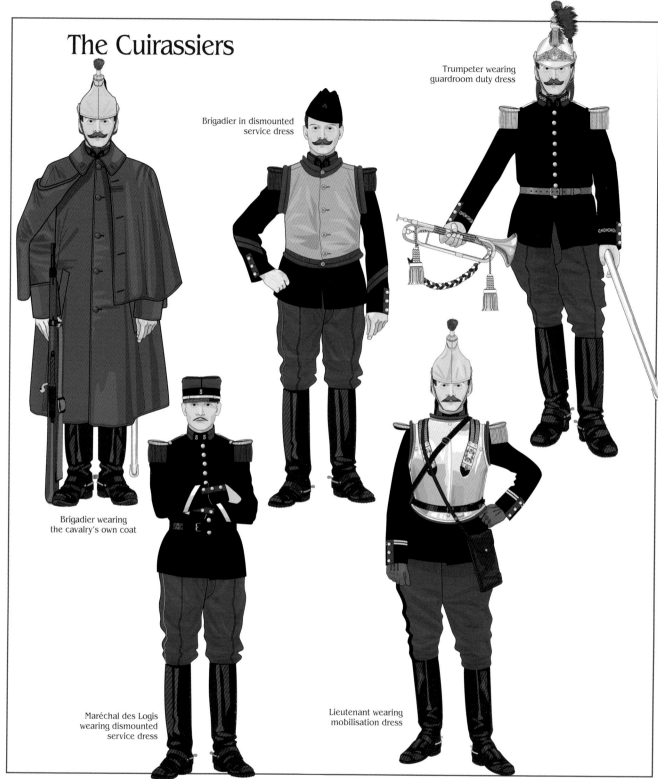

Trumpeter wearing
guardroom duty dress

Brigadier in dismounted
service dress

Brigadier wearing
the cavalry's own coat

Maréchal des Logis
wearing dismounted
service dress

Lieutenant wearing
mobilisation dress

22

The Dragoons

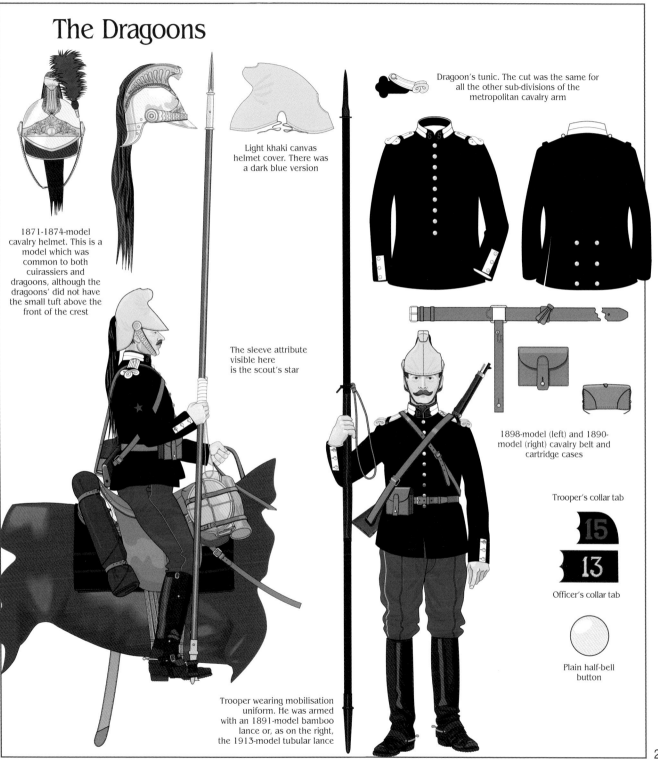

1871-1874-model cavalry helmet. This is a model which was common to both cuirassiers and dragoons, although the dragoons' did not have the small tuft above the front of the crest

Light khaki canvas helmet cover. There was a dark blue version

The sleeve attribute visible here is the scout's star

Trooper wearing mobilisation uniform. He was armed with an 1891-model bamboo lance or, as on the right, the 1913-model tubular lance

Dragoon's tunic. The cut was the same for all the other sub-divisions of the metropolitan cavalry arm

1898-model (left) and 1890-model (right) cavalry belt and cartridge cases

Trooper's collar tab

15

13

Officer's collar tab

Plain half-bell button

The Dragoons

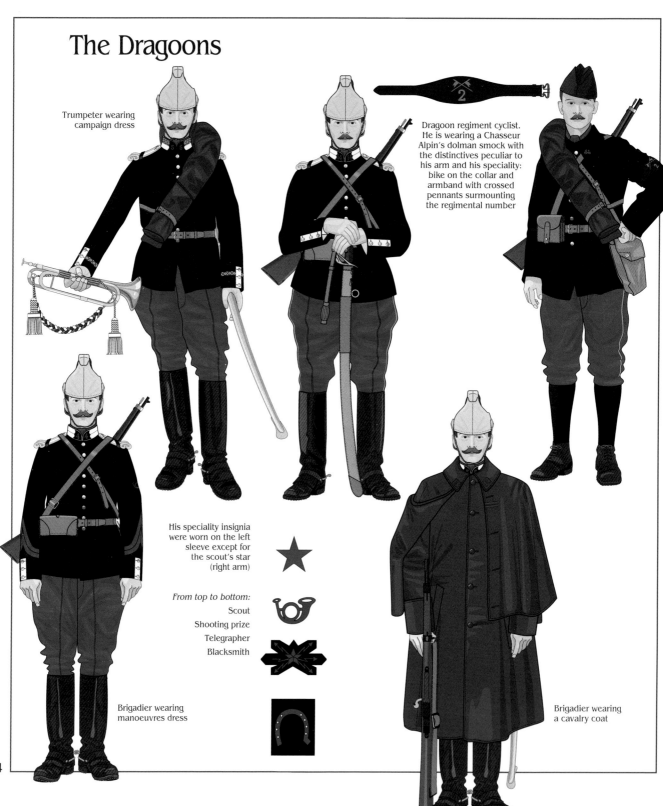

Trumpeter wearing campaign dress

Dragoon regiment cyclist. He is wearing a Chasseur Alpin's dolman smock with the distinctives peculiar to his arm and his speciality: bike on the collar and armband with crossed pennants surmounting the regimental number

His speciality insignia were worn on the left sleeve except for the scout's star (right arm)

From top to bottom:
Scout
Shooting prize
Telegrapher
Blacksmith

Brigadier wearing manoeuvres dress

Brigadier wearing a cavalry coat

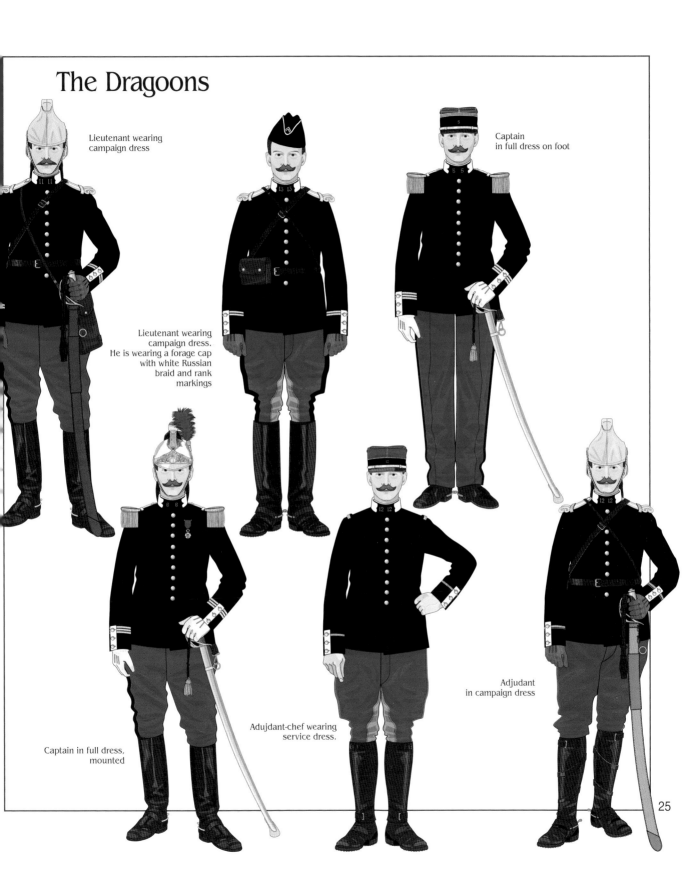

The Dragoons

Lieutenant wearing
campaign dress

Captain
in full dress on foot

Lieutenant wearing
campaign dress.
He is wearing a forage cap
with white Russian
braid and rank
markings

Adujdant-chef wearing
service dress.

Adjudant
in campaign dress

Captain in full dress,
mounted

The Chasseurs à cheval

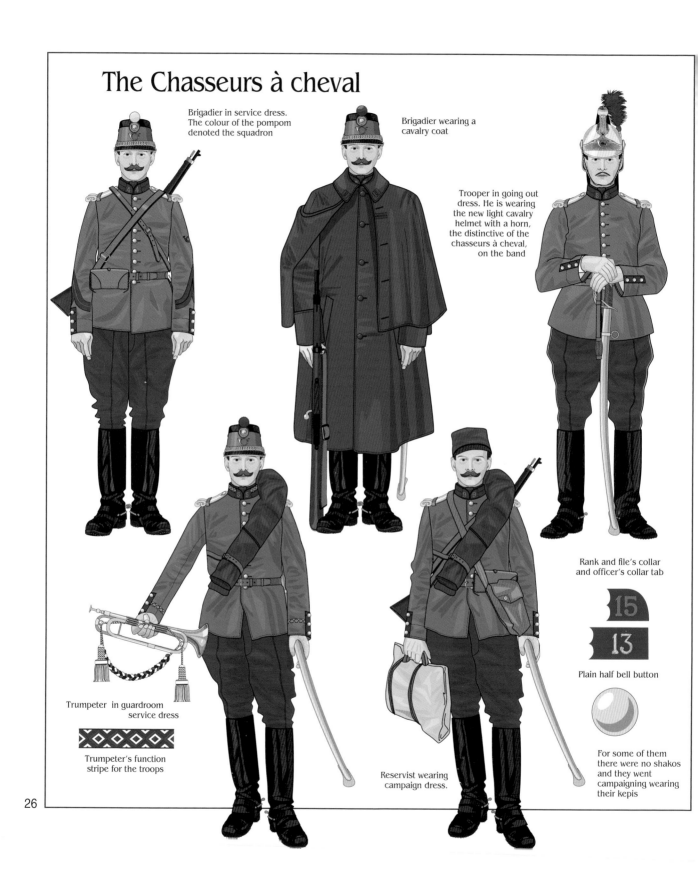

Brigadier in service dress. The colour of the pompom denoted the squadron

Brigadier wearing a cavalry coat

Trooper in going out dress. He is wearing the new light cavalry helmet with a horn, the distinctive of the chasseurs à cheval, on the band

Trumpeter in guardroom service dress

Trumpeter's function stripe for the troops

Reservist wearing campaign dress.

Rank and file's collar and officer's collar tab

15

13

Plain half bell button

For some of them there were no shakos and they went campaigning wearing their kepis

The Chasseurs à cheval

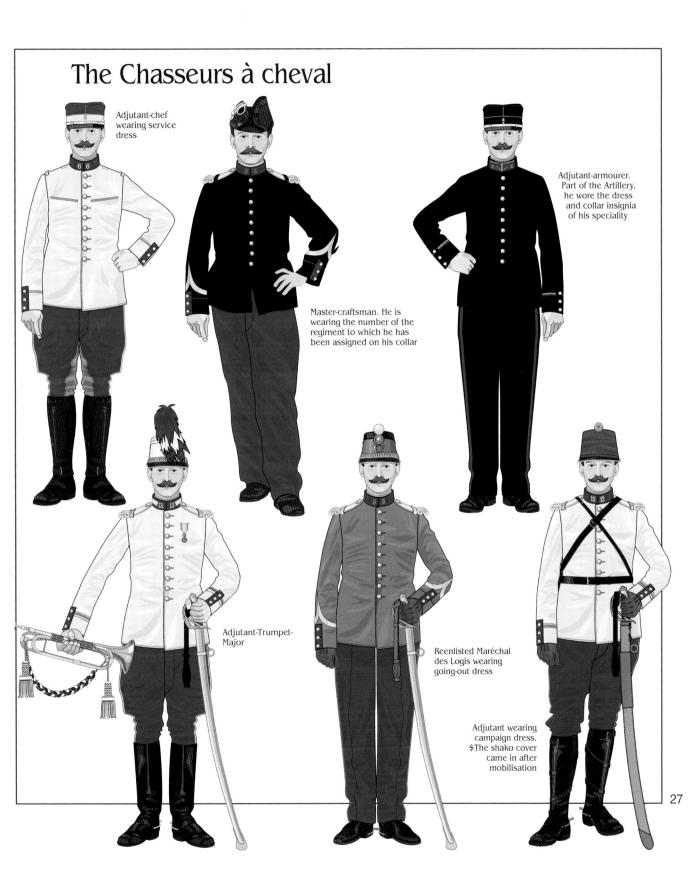

Adjutant-chef wearing service dress

Master-craftsman. He is wearing the number of the regiment to which he has been assigned on his collar

Adjutant-armourer. Part of the Artillery, he wore the dress and collar insignia of his speciality

Adjutant-Trumpet-Major

Reenlisted Maréchal des Logis wearing going-out dress

Adjutant wearing campaign dress. $The shako cover came in after mobilisation

27

The Chasseurs à cheval

Lieutenant wearing a
cavalry coat

Colonel wearing
full dress

Lieutenant wearing
a pelisse. This article
of clothing with its
astrakhan border
was worn only in winter
and meant rather a large
outlay for an officer
of this rank

Lieutenant wearing
mobilisation dress.
He could also wear
a tunic tailored from
the troops' cloth

Sabre gusset
for officer's
saddle

The Hussars

Reservist wearing mobilisation dress. This hussar is still wearing the old dolman with white tresses

Scout trooper wearing mobilisation uniform. Like soldiers from other arms wearing a red forage cap he is also wearing a blue canvas muff

Trumpeter wearing guardroom service dress

Territorial trooper wearing mobilisation dress. The packs and the weapons were the same as his brothers-in-arms in the active regiments. The number on his tunic collar indicate his regiment

Trooper wearing full dress, rear view

Trooper wearing full dress and a 1912-model helmet with the band star peculiar to the Hussars

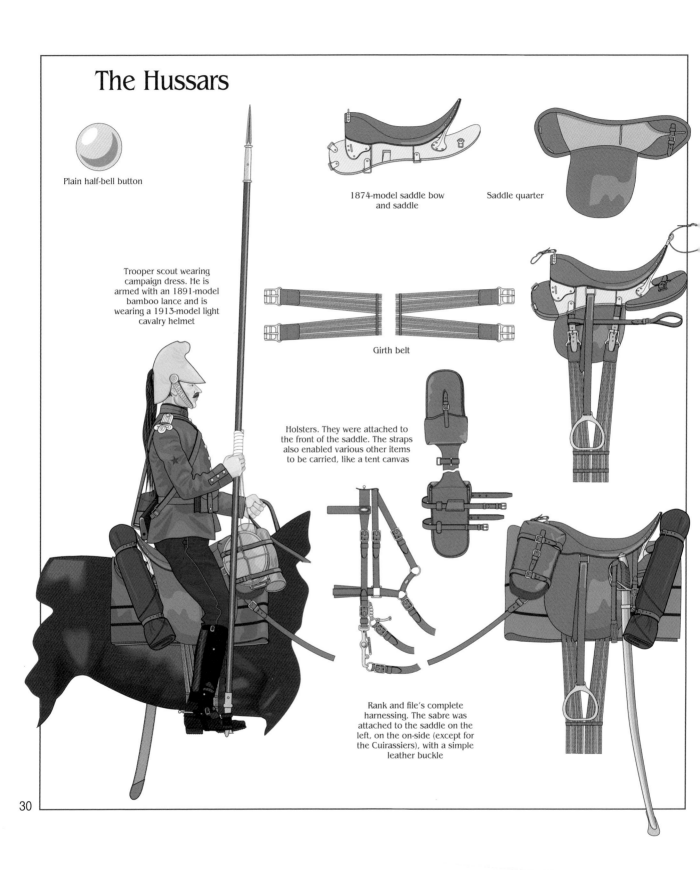

The Hussars

Plain half-bell button

1874-model saddle bow
and saddle

Saddle quarter

Trooper scout wearing
campaign dress. He is
armed with an 1891-model
bamboo lance and is
wearing a 1913-model light
cavalry helmet

Girth belt

Holsters. They were attached to
the front of the saddle. The straps
also enabled various other items
to be carried, like a tent canvas

Rank and file's complete
harnessing. The sabre was
attached to the saddle on the
left, on the on-side (except for
the Cuirassiers), with a simple
leather buckle

30

The Hussars

Lieutenant wearing
mobilisation uniform.
His tunic has been tailored
from the troops' cloth

Lieutenant wearing
manoeuvres dress

Captain wearing full
service dress
on foot

Saddle
and harness
for officers.
The coat was
rolled up into
a rubberised canvas sheath. The leather
bag was only worn when campaigning, just
like the saddle bags. The colonel
commanding the regiment had the same
harness, but his saddlecloth was decorated
with two stripes, the inner one
being narrower

Captain in full dress

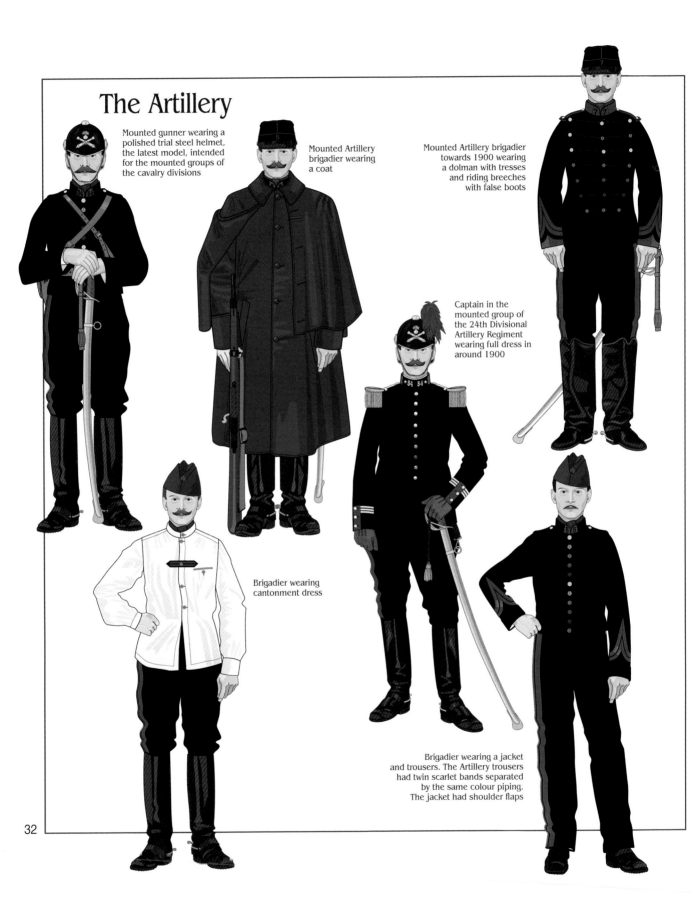

The Artillery

Mounted gunner wearing a polished trial steel helmet, the latest model, intended for the mounted groups of the cavalry divisions

Mounted Artillery brigadier wearing a coat

Mounted Artillery brigadier towards 1900 wearing a dolman with tresses and riding breeches with false boots

Captain in the mounted group of the 24th Divisional Artillery Regiment wearing full dress in around 1900

Brigadier wearing cantonment dress

Brigadier wearing a jacket and trousers. The Artillery trousers had twin scarlet bands separated by the same colour piping. The jacket had shoulder flaps

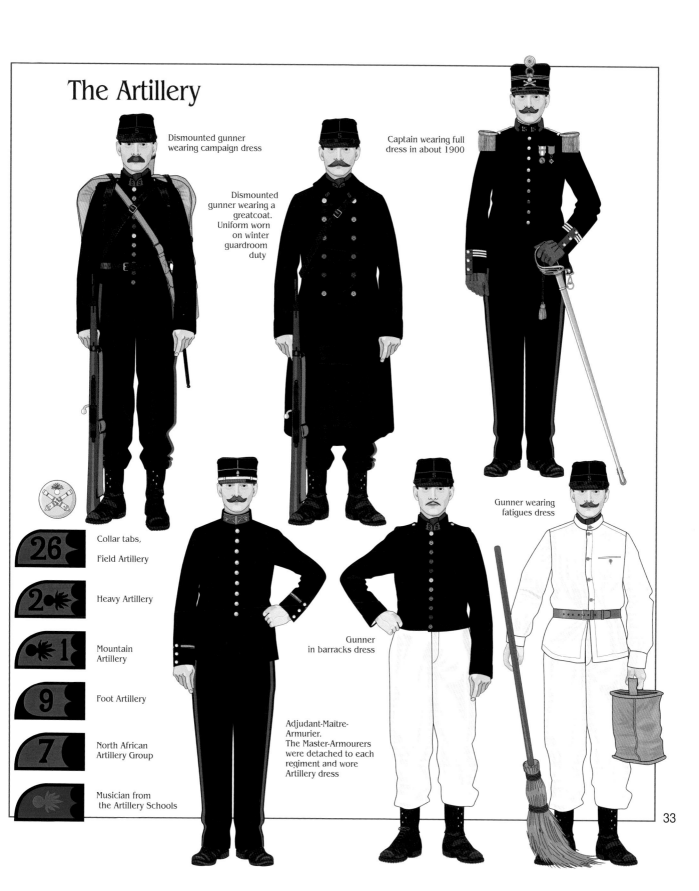

The Artillery

Dismounted gunner wearing campaign dress

Dismounted gunner wearing a greatcoat. Uniform worn on winter guardroom duty

Captain wearing full dress in about 1900

Collar tabs,

Field Artillery

26

Heavy Artillery

2

Mountain Artillery

1

Foot Artillery

9

North African Artillery Group

7

Musician from the Artillery Schools

Gunner in barracks dress

Adjudant-Maitre-Armurier. The Master-Armourers were detached to each regiment and wore Artillery dress

Gunner wearing fatigues dress

33

The Mountain Artillery

Mule driver.
The Mountain Artillery gunners wore a rather mixed-up uniform, borrowing different characteristic elements from the mountain troops: a beret decorated with a scarlet grenade, blue wool belt and leggings

In 1909, the mountain artillery batteries were regrouped in two mountain artillery regiments stationed in Grenoble and Nice. A regiment comprised six batteries of 65-mm 1906-model quick-firing cannon

Trumpeter, 1st Class wearing summer dress

Maréchal des Logis Chef wearing going out dress

Brigadier wearing jacket and trousers. The trousers have been embellished with a double scarlet band separated by the same colour piping

Lieutenant wearing campaign dress

The Engineers

-Corporal wearing summer manoeuvres dress

Sapper wearing summer manoeuvres dress and a raw linen blouse

Salaried clerk from the 5th Génie. He was nicknamed the "corporal till midday" because he only wore stripes on one sleeve. On his collar is the railways insignia

Speciality insignia for the railways, troops and NCOs. Collar tab and button for the rank and file and officers

Sapper wearing barracks dress

Corporal in mobilisation dress. He is armed with an 1886/93-model Lebel rifle. However certain regiments were issued with musketoons

The Engineers and Balloonists

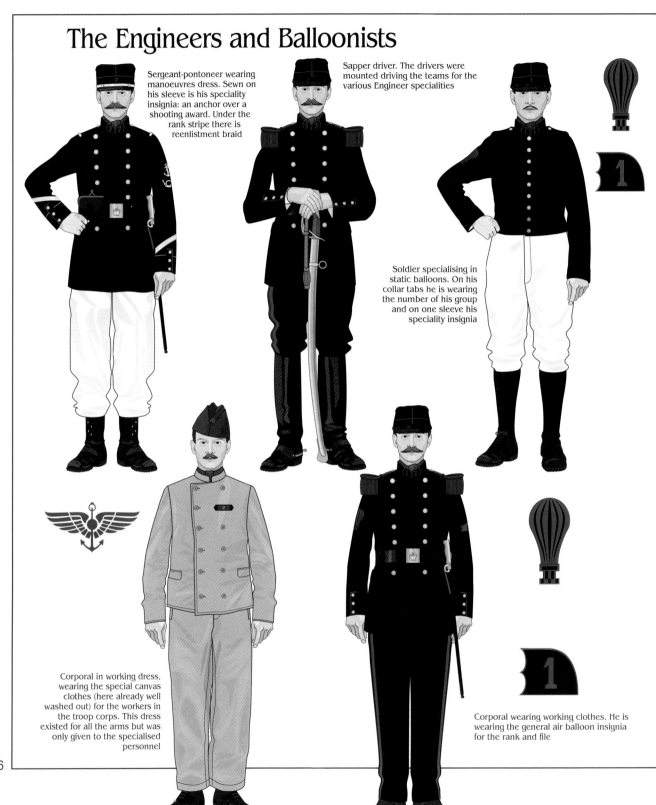

Sergeant-pontoneer wearing manoeuvres dress. Sewn on his sleeve is his speciality insignia: an anchor over a shooting award. Under the rank stripe there is reenlistment braid

Sapper driver. The drivers were mounted driving the teams for the various Engineer specialities

Soldier specialising in static balloons. On his collar tabs he is wearing the number of his group and on one sleeve his speciality insignia

Corporal in working dress, wearing the special canvas clothes (here already well washed out) for the workers in the troop corps. This dress existed for all the arms but was only given to the specialised personnel

Corporal wearing working clothes. He is wearing the general air balloon insignia for the rank and file

Air Balloons

From top to bottom:
Mechanic.
Certificated mechanic
Certificated mechanic
(NCO)

Uniform buttons

Specialist balloon anchorer

Air Balloon soldier. Sewn
on his right sleeve is the
general insignia

Sergeant with general
insignia and NCO's
collar tab

Air Balloon corporal

Air Balloon captain wearing
full dress towards 1910

Captain. He is wearing
the Air Balloon
armband on his 1913-
model smock

Military Aviation

Soldier,
1st Class Aviation

Aircraft
mechanic's
collar tab

Pilot's collar tab
(troop)

Corporal mechanic
in working clothes

NCO's armband

Pilot.
Reconstitution
made using a
photograph by
Adolphe Pégoud

Pilot-Sergeant
wearing a dolman
smock

Infantry officer's
button

Aviation Captain
wearing full dress
towards 1910

Officer in flying
gear. He has
donned a Paris
fireman's leather
jacket with the
Military Aviation
armband and is
wearing a Roold
helmet

The Supply Train

Captain wearing full dress, dismounted

Uniform button

The team train was a logistics arm used for military transport. It was responsible for moving most of the supplies particularly food (on behalf of the Intendancy Service) as well as all medical service transportation

Captain wearing campaign dress

Lieutenant wearing manoeuvres dress

Brigadier wearing winter guard duty dress

Maréchal des Logis wearing service dress

Driver wearing campaign dress

The Gendarmerie

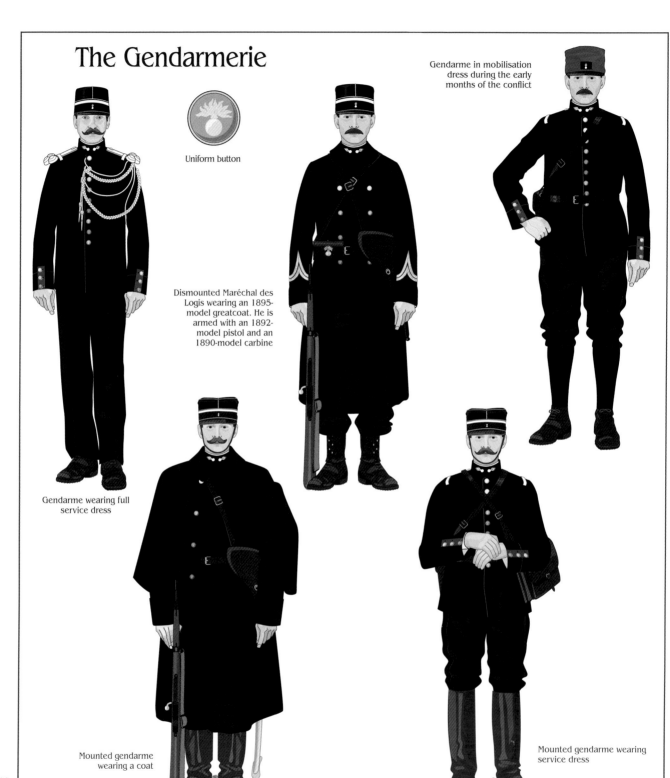

Uniform button

Gendarme in mobilisation dress during the early months of the conflict

Dismounted Maréchal des Logis wearing an 1895-model greatcoat. He is armed with an 1892-model pistol and an 1890-model carbine

Gendarme wearing full service dress

Mounted gendarme wearing a coat

Mounted gendarme wearing service dress

The Gendarmerie

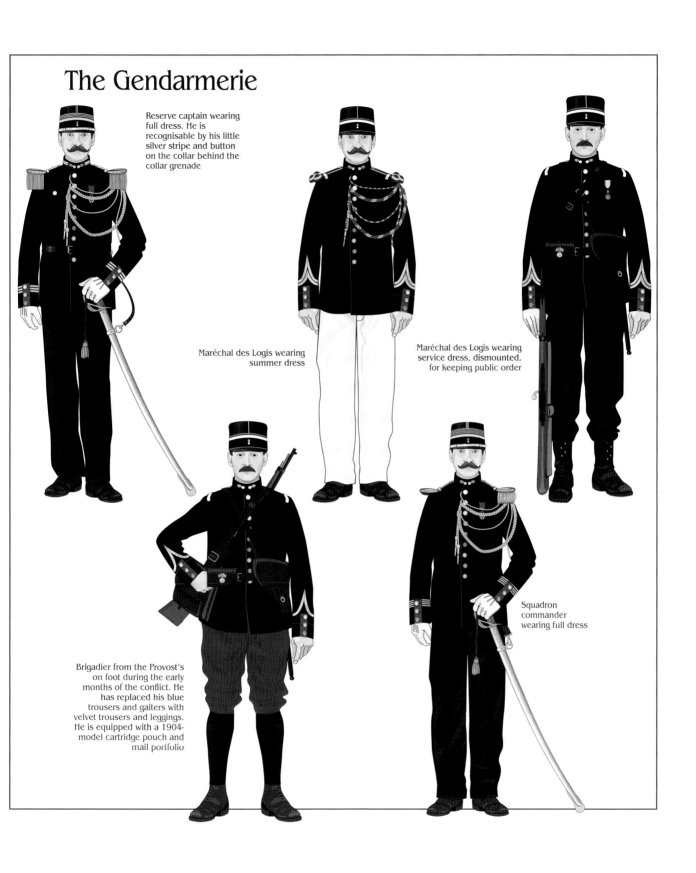

Reserve captain wearing full dress. He is recognisable by his little silver stripe and button on the collar behind the collar grenade

Maréchal des Logis wearing summer dress

Maréchal des Logis wearing service dress, dismounted, for keeping public order

Brigadier from the Provost's on foot during the early months of the conflict. He has replaced his blue trousers and gaiters with velvet trousers and leggings. He is equipped with a 1904-model cartridge pouch and mail portfolio

Squadron commander wearing full dress

Quartermaster, Administration, Staff Secretariat

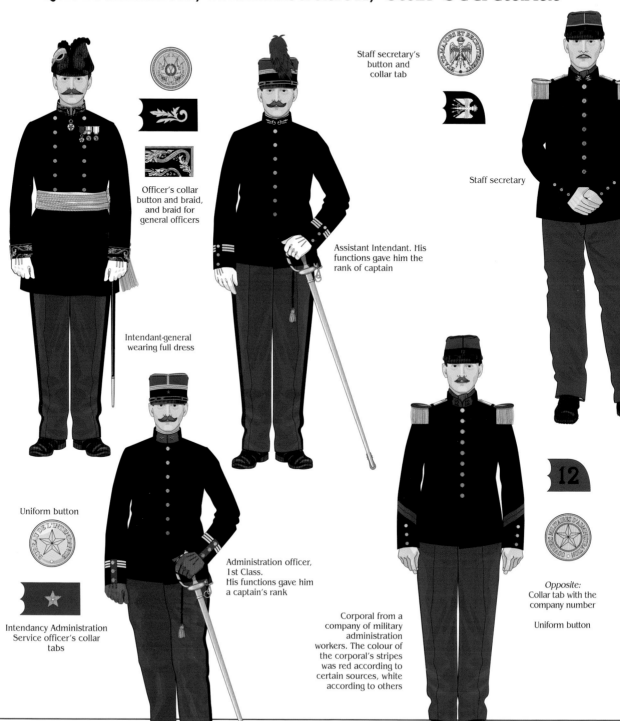

Staff secretary's button and collar tab

Officer's collar button and braid, and braid for general officers

Staff secretary

Assistant Intendant. His functions gave him the rank of captain

Intendant-general wearing full dress

Uniform button

Administration officer, 1st Class. His functions gave him a captain's rank

Intendancy Administration Service officer's collar tabs

Corporal from a company of military administration workers. The colour of the corporal's stripes was red according to certain sources, white according to others

Opposite:
Collar tab with the company number

Uniform button

Military Telegraphs, Treasury and Postal Services, Almoners

Military Telegraphy

Officer and NCO in about 1910.
As a distinctive they wore a star
with lightning flashes on their
collar tabs and uniform buttons.
The officer is wearing his sous-
lieutenant's stripe like the
Artillery, rather than wearing
it as chevron

Personnel armband.

TRÉSORERIE
ET
POSTES

Chest cross worn
by the army
almoners

Army almoner

Army Treasury
and Postal Service
sub-agent

Army Treasury and Postal
Service officer.
These officers wore
uniforms only
in the case of mobilisation

Collar tab and
uniform button of the
Army Treasury and
Postal Service

The Medical and Veterinary Services

Doctor-Major, 1st Class. He had the rank of major. He could be responsible for a corps' medical service. Certain doctors still wore the dolman tunic on mobilisation

Médecin-Aide-Major (Assistant Doctor-Major), 2nd Class wearing mobilisation dress. He is wearing a 1913-model smock. He had sous-lieutenant rank

Pharmacien-Aide-Major, 1st Class wearing full dress towards 1900. The velvet kepi band was the colour of the service, i.e. green

Soldier, 1st class from a section of military nurses wearing mobilisation dress. The nurses were armed with a revolver and an obsolete 1866-model bayonet. Like all the Medical Service personnel, they wore a Red Cross armband giving them neutral status

Military Nurses Section

Medical Corps (officers)

Veterinary Service officer's collar tabs and button

Veterinary-Aide-Major, 1st Class wearing mobilisation dress. On his collar he is wearing the specific garnet velvet tabs with the sage flower leaf motif and silver buttons on his tunic

Geneva Convention armbands, regulation (above) and a simplified variant

44

The Zouaves

Corporal and soldier from the 2nd Zouaves wearing full dress in around 1910

Bugler from the 2nd Zouaves wearing full dress in about 1910.
A white turban was rolled around the chechia. Like his brothers-in-arms in the ranks, he is wearing white gaiters

Bugler from the 2nd Zouaves on mobilisation.
Like the rest of the rank and file, he could cover his headgear with a blue sleeve in order to make it less visible

Corporal wearing manoeuvres dress. The fact that he is wearing a flax blouse shows that they were summer manoeuvres

The Zouaves

Zouave corporal's and Zouave's uniforms at the time of mobilisation

Jacket from the 1st Zouaves with the jonquil tombo

Chechia and its tassel

Waistcoat. It buttoned up on the side

Individual mess tin, *bouthéon* (cooking pot) and 2-litre (4-pint) flask

Blue woollen belt worn under the jacket

Equipment worn by the Zouaves with their specific dorsal cartridge case. The jacket was worn over it, covering the straps

Saroua.

Puttees and boots

46

The Zouaves

Corporal-drummer wearing summer manoeuvres dress

Corporal wearing fatigues

Plain half-bell button

Sous-lieutenant wearing campaign dress. On his belt he is carrying a map-case and a pair of binoculars

Sergeant-major wearing campaign dress. He was – like in the metropolitan infantry – armed with an 1892-model revolver and an NCO's sabre

Sous-lieutenant wearing full dress. On the officer's uniform, note the slash on the rear of the sleeves formed by little bell buttons, and the baggy trousers peculiar to the Army of Africa

The Algerian Tirailleurs

Tirailleur corporal
in full parade dress

Tirailleur wearing
campaign dress

Corporal in campaign
dress. Like with
the Zouaves,
on mobilisation
he was issued with
a blue chechia cover

Corporal in full dress.
As with the Zouaves,
the buglers'
and the drummers'
function stripe
appeared at the top
of the jacket,
and above the facings

The Algerian Tirailleurs

Bugler and drum-corporal wearing campaign dress

Sergeant-major in campaign dress. He is carrying the same weapons as his Zouave counterpart

Plain half-bell button

Staff brevet-captain in about 1890. He is wearing a dolman-smock and an aglet, the insignia of his function on a brigade's or division's staff

Lieutenant wearing winter uniform. In all the arms, the officers wore a pelisse cut in the same way and edged with astrakhan. Only the colour of the arm varied

The Tirailleurs

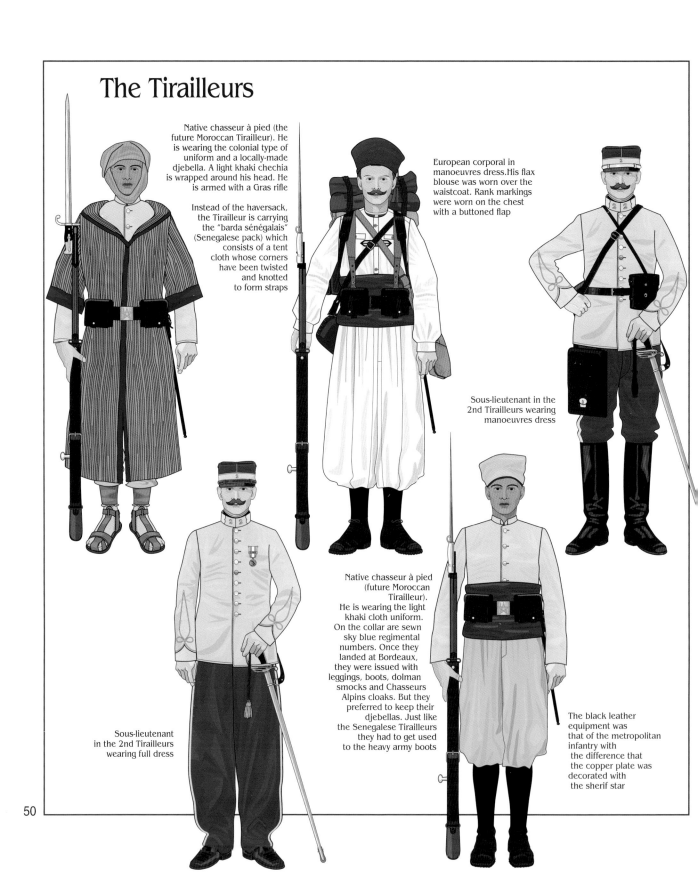

Native chasseur à pied (the future Moroccan Tirailleur). He is wearing the colonial type of uniform and a locally-made djebella. A light khaki chechia is wrapped around his head. He is armed with a Gras rifle

Instead of the haversack, the Tirailleur is carrying the "barda sénégalais" (Senegalese pack) which consists of a tent cloth whose corners have been twisted and knotted to form straps

European corporal in manoeuvres dress. His flax blouse was worn over the waistcoat. Rank markings were worn on the chest with a buttoned flap

Sous-lieutenant in the 2nd Tirailleurs wearing manoeuvres dress

Sous-lieutenant in the 2nd Tirailleurs wearing full dress

Native chasseur à pied (future Moroccan Tirailleur). He is wearing the light khaki cloth uniform. On the collar are sewn sky blue regimental numbers. Once they landed at Bordeaux, they were issued with leggings, boots, dolman smocks and Chasseurs Alpins cloaks. But they preferred to keep their djebellas. Just like the Senegalese Tirailleurs they had to get used to the heavy army boots

The black leather equipment was that of the metropolitan infantry with the difference that the copper plate was decorated with the sherif star

50

The African Chasseurs

Chasseur in fatigues. For campaign and full dress, the African Chasseurs wore a *taconnet*, a "cousin" of the light cavalry's shako. In off-duty and going out dress they wore a madder red chechia decorated with three black bands. The silk tassel attached to the top of the chechia was the colour of the squadron like the pompom on the taconnet

Chasseur driver for supply carts and pack animals

Brigadier wearing campaign dress

Dismounted trooper wearing campaign dress

Brigadier-trumpeter from the 5th RCA in about 1905

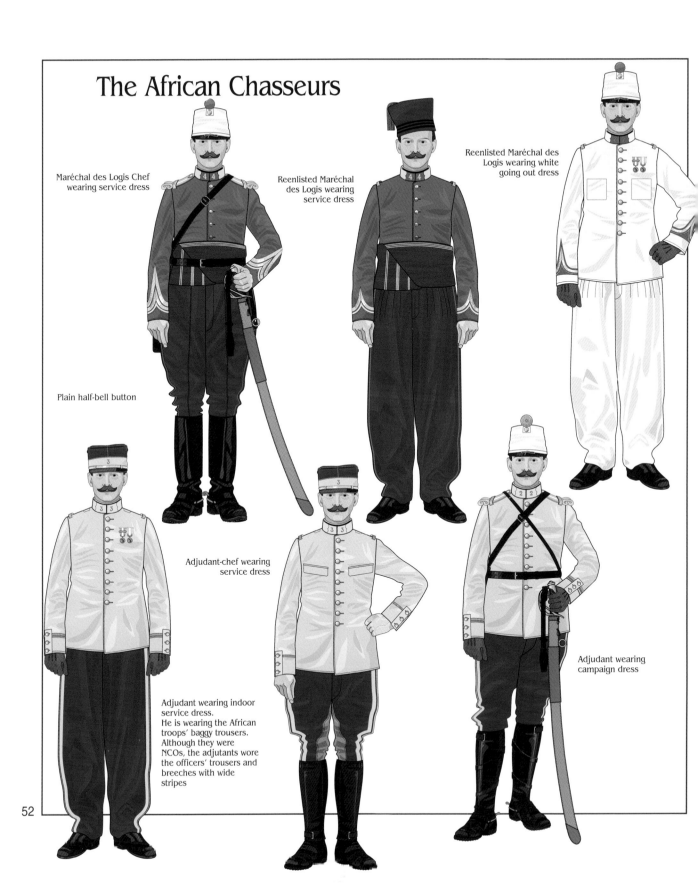

The African Chasseurs

Maréchal des Logis Chef
wearing service dress

Reenlisted Maréchal
des Logis wearing
service dress

Reenlisted Maréchal des
Logis wearing white
going out dress

Plain half-bell button

Adjudant-chef wearing
service dress

Adjudant wearing
campaign dress

Adjudant wearing indoor
service dress.
He is wearing the African
troops' baggy trousers.
Although they were
NCOs, the adjudants wore
the officers' trousers and
breeches with wide
stripes

The African Chasseurs

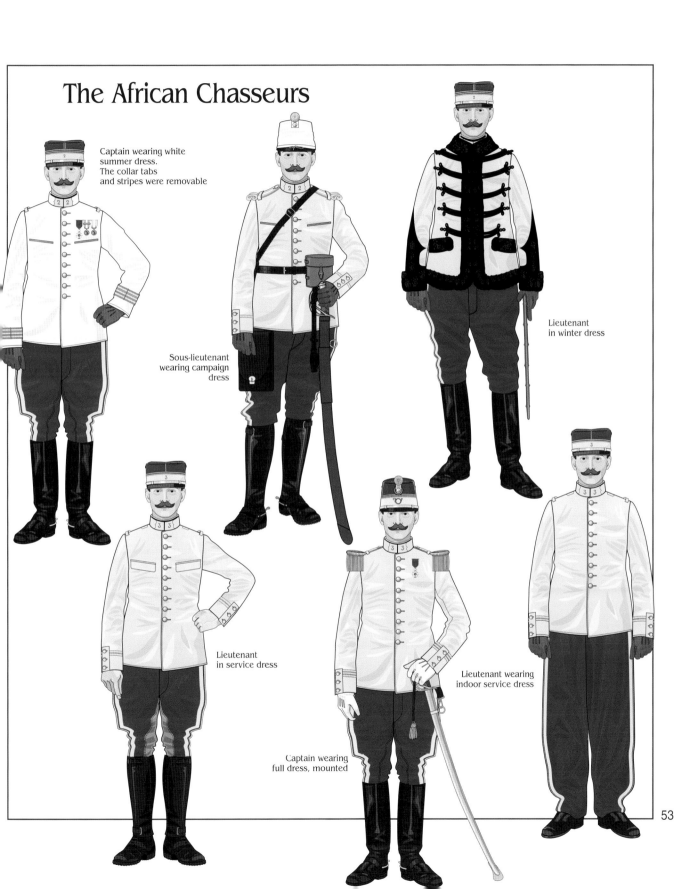

Captain wearing white summer dress. The collar tabs and stripes were removable

Sous-lieutenant wearing campaign dress

Lieutenant in winter dress

Lieutenant in service dress

Captain wearing full dress, mounted

Lieutenant wearing indoor service dress

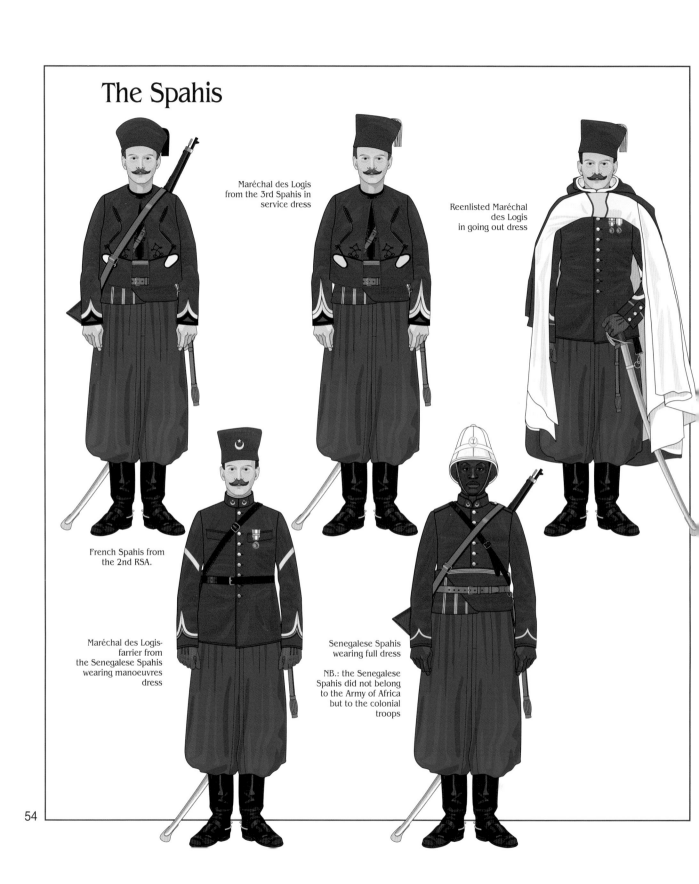

The Spahis

Maréchal des Logis from the 3rd Spahis in service dress

Reenlisted Maréchal des Logis in going out dress

French Spahis from the 2nd RSA.

Maréchal des Logis-farrier from the Senegalese Spahis wearing manoeuvres dress

Senegalese Spahis wearing full dress

NB.: the Senegalese Spahis did not belong to the Army of Africa but to the colonial troops

The Algerian Spahis

French trumpeter from the 3rd Spahis. The French Spahis wore a madder red chechia and soft boots as distinctives. The uniform was introduced in 1902 at a time when the function stripes were brought back again. It seems that at that date the trumpeters wore a white and sky blue burnous, but this cannot be confirmed categorically

Native Spahi from the 4th Regiment. Unlike his French counterpart, he is wearing soft boots (khoffes) slipped into low black leather shoes. His headgear consists of the genhour, covered with the haïck. This is kept in place by a 30-foot camel hair rope. The remainder of the uniform was the same as the rest of the French native troops. The manner of carrying the carbine over the burnous was peculiar to the native troopers.

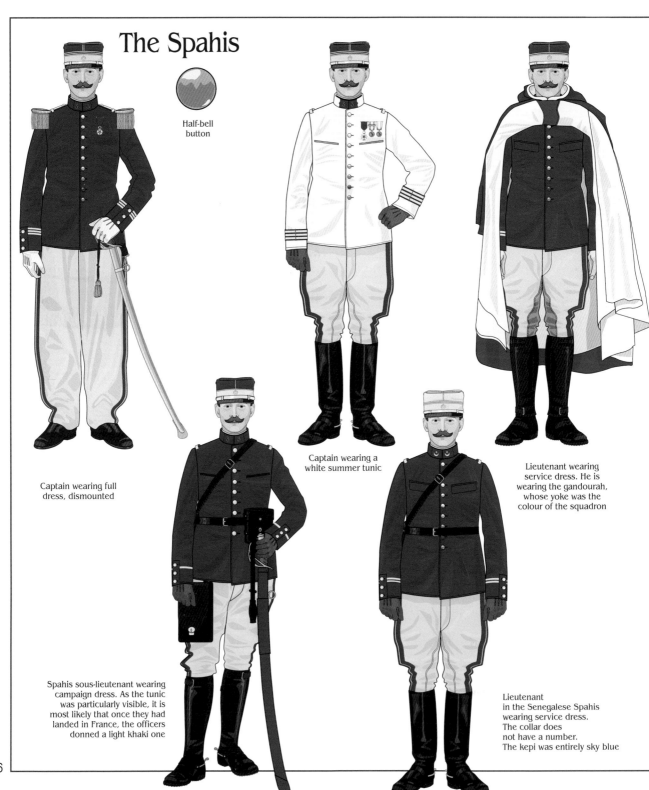

The Spahis

Half-bell
button

Captain wearing full
dress, dismounted

Captain wearing a
white summer tunic

Lieutenant wearing
service dress. He is
wearing the gandourah,
whose yoke was the
colour of the squadron

Spahis sous-lieutenant wearing
campaign dress. As the tunic
was particularly visible, it is
most likely that once they had
landed in France, the officers
donned a light khaki one

Lieutenant
in the Senegalese Spahis
wearing service dress.
The collar does
not have a number.
The kepi was entirely sky blue

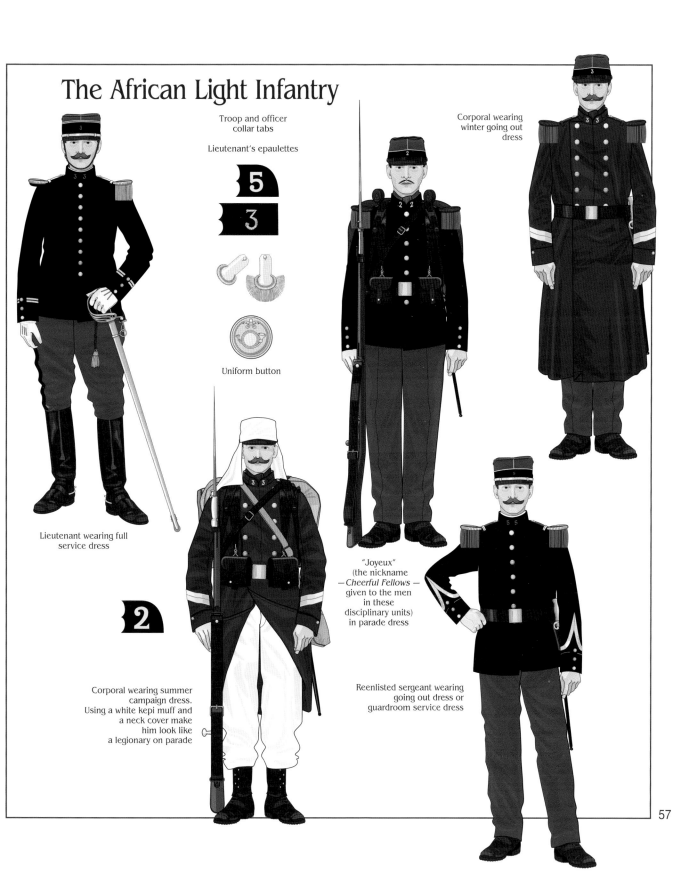

The African Light Infantry

Troop and officer collar tabs

Lieutenant's epaulettes

Uniform button

Lieutenant wearing full service dress

Corporal wearing summer campaign dress. Using a white kepi muff and a neck cover make him look like a legionary on parade

"Joyeux" (the nickname —*Cheerful Fellows*— given to the men in these disciplinary units) in parade dress

Corporal wearing winter going out dress

Reenlisted sergeant wearing going out dress or guardroom service dress

The Foreign Legion

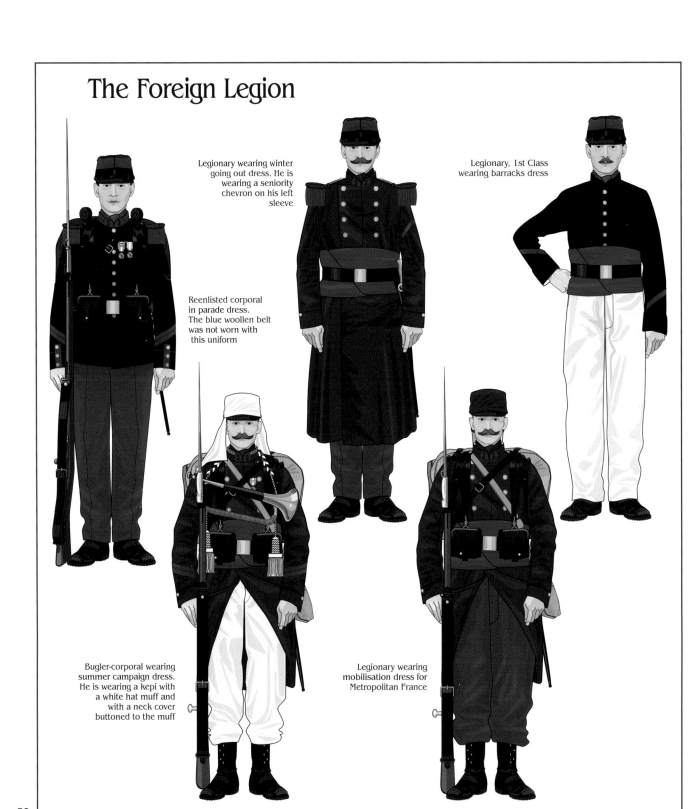

Legionary wearing winter going out dress. He is wearing a seniority chevron on his left sleeve

Legionary, 1st Class wearing barracks dress

Reenlisted corporal in parade dress. The blue woollen belt was not worn with this uniform

Bugler-corporal wearing summer campaign dress. He is wearing a kepi with a white hat muff and with a neck cover buttoned to the muff

Legionary wearing mobilisation dress for Metropolitan France

The Foreign Legion

Captain wearing full service dress

Legionary, 1st Class wearing light khaki uniform, the same as the colonial troops. Note the facing line underlined by blue braid

Corporal wearing Far-East going out dress. In Indochina the Legion used the colonial infantry's overcoat

Corporal wearing campaign dress for Morocco in about 1907

Lieutenant wearing mobilisation dress

From top to bottom:
Collar tab off a greatcoat and troops cloth uniform

Officer's collar tab

The Colonial Infantry

Soldier wearing full dress, Far-East, towards 1910. He is wearing an 1890 -model topee, made of cork and covered with white cloth and decorated with a brass Navy anchor which shows that the colonial troops belonged to the Admiralty before 1900

NB. Soldiers in the Colonial Infantry were nicknamed the "marsouins" (porpoise)

Corporal wearing summer going out dress

Soldier wearing full dress towards 1910. The belt was fastened by means of a flat, square wide buckle and not with a plate. This buckle was peculiar to the colonial troops and the Navy from which they were derived

Soldier wearing barracks dress

Far-East Corporal Nurse

Cyclist from a Colonial Infantry regiment

The Colonial Infantry

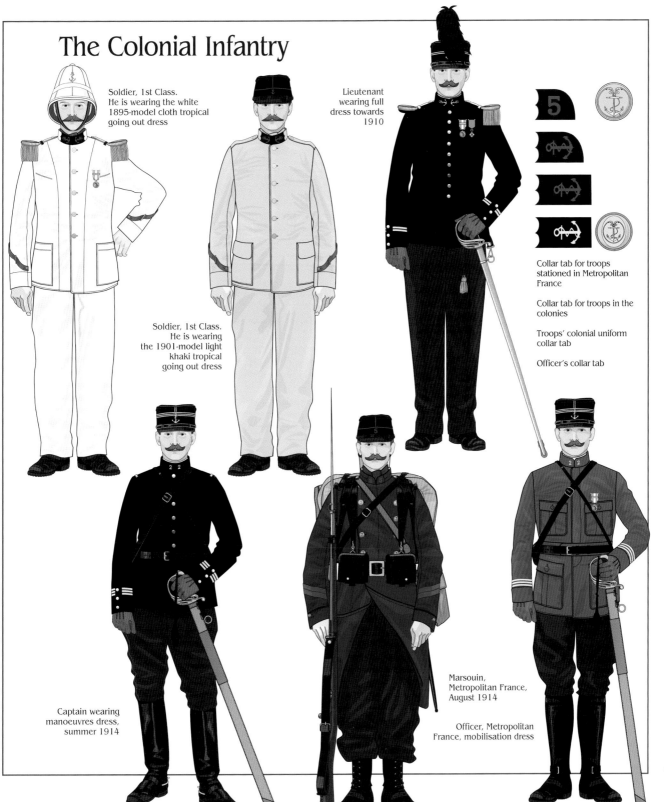

Soldier, 1st Class. He is wearing the white 1895-model cloth tropical going out dress

Soldier, 1st Class. He is wearing the 1901-model light khaki tropical going out dress

Lieutenant wearing full dress towards 1910

Collar tab for troops stationed in Metropolitan France

Collar tab for troops in the colonies

Troops' colonial uniform collar tab

Officer's collar tab

Captain wearing manoeuvres dress, summer 1914

Marsouin, Metropolitan France, August 1914

Officer, Metropolitan France, mobilisation dress

The Senegalese and Malagasy Tirailleurs

Senegalese Tirailleur
wearing cloth uniform
towards 1900

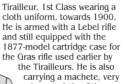

Collar tab for the troops,
particular to the
Senegalese and Malagasy
Tirailleurs. The latter
were not in France
during the early months
of the Great War

Tirailleur, 1st Class wearing a
cloth uniform, towards 1900.
He is armed with a Lebel rifle
and still equipped with the
1877-model cartridge case for
the Gras rifle used earlier by
the Tirailleurs. He is also
carrying a machete, very
characteristic of the
colonial tirailleurs

Tirailleur officer.
He in fact belongs to the
Colonial Infantry whose
distinctives he has
retained

Tirailleur wearing
the new 1914-
model overcoat.
This complete
uniform with
leggings and boots
was not worn
before mid-1915

Tirailleur sergeant wearing
parade dress towards 1913.
It was in this dress that the
continental French
discovered the Senegalese
Tirailleurs on 14 July 1914
at Longchamp

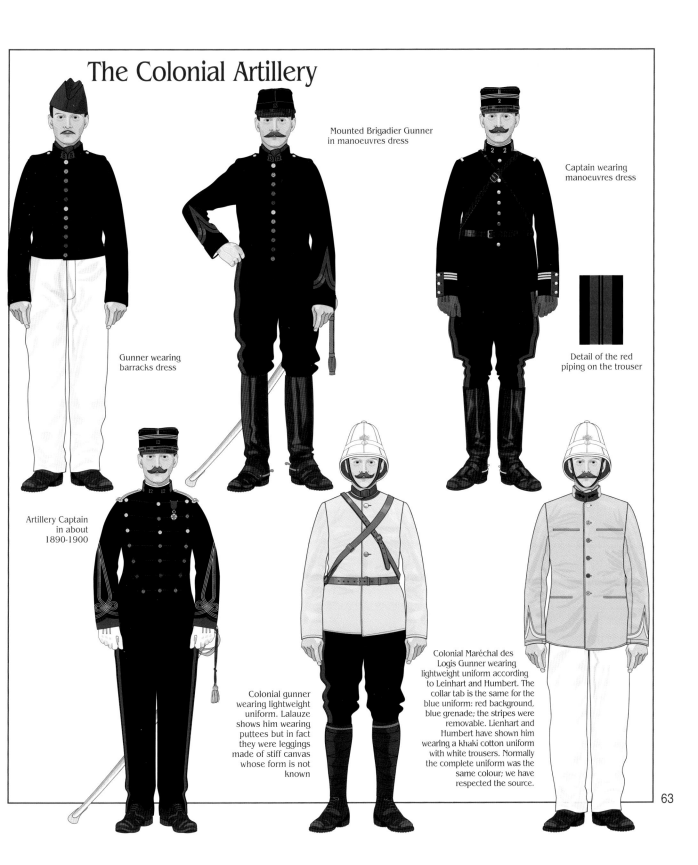

The Colonial Artillery

Gunner wearing
barracks dress

Mounted Brigadier Gunner
in manoeuvres dress

Captain wearing
manoeuvres dress

Detail of the red
piping on the trouser

Artillery Captain
in about
1890-1900

Colonial gunner
wearing lightweight
uniform. Lalauze
shows him wearing
puttees but in fact
they were leggings
made of stiff canvas
whose form is not
known

Colonial Maréchal des
Logis Gunner wearing
lightweight uniform according
to Leinhart and Humbert. The
collar tab is the same for the
blue uniform: red background,
blue grenade; the stripes were
removable. Lienhart and
Humbert have shown him
wearing a khaki cotton uniform
with white trousers. Normally
the complete uniform was the
same colour; we have
respected the source.

The Sailors and Marines

Second-master wearing service dress

Button

Sailor wearing guard dress

Bugler wearing campaign dress at mobilisation. On a period picture, the function stripes can be seen sewn on the bottom of the sleeves of the greatcoat. This stripe did not appear on the other corps' greatcoats

Sailor wearing winter going out dress

Quartermaster wearing campaign dress at mobilisation. Although rarely seen on period photographs, it would seem that the collar of the smock was worn over that of the greatcoat

Second-master wearing campaign dress at mobilisation

French Army Corps in 1914

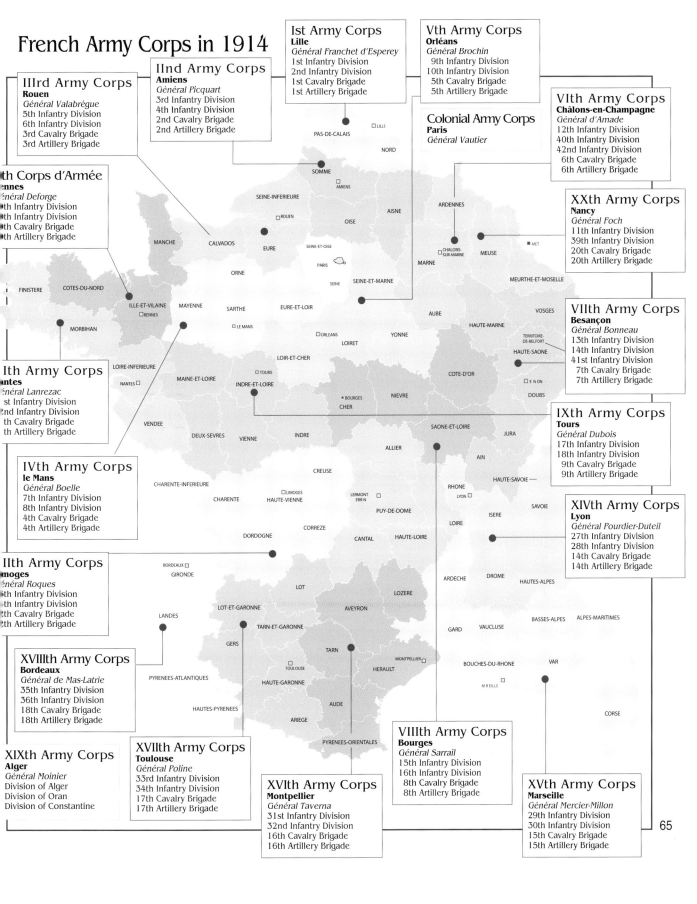

IIIrd Army Corps
Rouen
Général Valabrègue
5th Infantry Division
6th Infantry Division
3rd Cavalry Brigade
3rd Artillery Brigade

IInd Army Corps
Amiens
Général Picquart
3rd Infantry Division
4th Infantry Division
2nd Cavalry Brigade
2nd Artillery Brigade

Ist Army Corps
Lille
Général Franchet d'Esperey
1st Infantry Division
2nd Infantry Division
1st Cavalry Brigade
1st Artillery Brigade

Vth Army Corps
Orléans
Général Brochin
9th Infantry Division
10th Infantry Division
5th Cavalry Brigade
5th Artillery Brigade

Colonial Army Corps
Paris
Général Vautier

VIth Army Corps
Châlons-en-Champagne
Général d'Amade
12th Infantry Division
40th Infantry Division
42nd Infantry Division
6th Cavalry Brigade
6th Artillery Brigade

XXth Army Corps
Nancy
Général Foch
11th Infantry Division
39th Infantry Division
20th Cavalry Brigade
20th Artillery Brigade

Xth Corps d'Armée
Rennes
Général Deforge
Xth Infantry Division
Xth Infantry Division
Xth Cavalry Brigade
Xth Artillery Brigade

VIIth Army Corps
Besançon
Général Bonneau
13th Infantry Division
14th Infantry Division
41st Infantry Division
7th Cavalry Brigade
7th Artillery Brigade

XIth Army Corps
Nantes
Général Lanrezac
Xst Infantry Division
Xnd Infantry Division
Xth Cavalry Brigade
Xth Artillery Brigade

IXth Army Corps
Tours
Général Dubois
17th Infantry Division
18th Infantry Division
9th Cavalry Brigade
9th Artillery Brigade

IVth Army Corps
le Mans
Général Boelle
7th Infantry Division
8th Infantry Division
4th Cavalry Brigade
4th Artillery Brigade

XIVth Army Corps
Lyon
Général Pourdier-Duteil
27th Infantry Division
28th Infantry Division
14th Cavalry Brigade
14th Artillery Brigade

XIIth Army Corps
Limoges
Général Roques
Xth Infantry Division
Xth Infantry Division
Xth Cavalry Brigade
Xth Artillery Brigade

XVIIIth Army Corps
Bordeaux
Général de Mas-Latrie
35th Infantry Division
36th Infantry Division
18th Cavalry Brigade
18th Artillery Brigade

XIXth Army Corps
Alger
Général Moinier
Division of Alger
Division of Oran
Division of Constantine

XVIIth Army Corps
Toulouse
Général Poline
33rd Infantry Division
34th Infantry Division
17th Cavalry Brigade
17th Artillery Brigade

XVIth Army Corps
Montpellier
Général Taverna
31st Infantry Division
32nd Infantry Division
16th Cavalry Brigade
16th Artillery Brigade

VIIIth Army Corps
Bourges
Général Sarrail
15th Infantry Division
16th Infantry Division
8th Cavalry Brigade
8th Artillery Brigade

XVth Army Corps
Marseille
Général Mercier-Millon
29th Infantry Division
30th Infantry Division
15th Cavalry Brigade
15th Artillery Brigade

65

BIBLIOGRAPHY and SOURCES

— Carnets de la Sabretache. Special numbers devoted to:
- Spahis
- African Chasseurs
- Zouaves
- Algerian tirailleurs
- Navy
- Air Force
- The year 1914

— Les uniformes de l'armée française 1914-1945 by François Vauvillier, auto-édition

— La cavalerie légère by Louis Delpérier, Éditions du Canonnier

— Soldats de 1914-1918 Édition Hachette

— L'uniforme et les armes des soldats de 1914-1918, Lilliane & Fred Funcken, Éditions Castermann

— Militaria magazine Collection

— Uniformes magazine Collection

- Les Chasseurs d'Afrique by Jacques Sicard and François Vauvillier, Histoire & Collections

- La Garde Rouge de Dakar by P. Rosière,

- Les Gardes d'Honneur

— La Grande Guerre de 1914-1918, by Marc Neuville, Les collections du Musée de l'Armée

— Musée du Mémorial de Verdun Collections

— Musée de l'Armée Collections

— Musée du Fort de la Pompelle (Reims) Collections

— Fanfare et musique des troupes à cheval, by Commandant Bucquoy, Éditions Jacques Grancher

— Les zouaves et tirailleurs by Jean-Louis Larcade, Éditions des Argonautes

— L'armée française en 1914 by Laurent Mirouze and S. Dkerle, Verlag

AKNOWLEDGEMENTS

We would like to thank Louis Delpérier, François Vauvillier, Denis Gandilhon and Jean-Louis Viau for their precious help, both morale-wise and publishing-wise.

Design, creation, lay-out and realisation by ANDRE JOUINEAU and JEAN-MARIE MONGIN.
© Histoire & Collections 2008
Computer Drawings by André JOUINEAU

All rights reserved. No part of this publication can be transmitted or reproduced without the written consent of the Author and the Publisher

ISBN : 978-2-35250-104-6

Publish number: 35250

Published by
HISTOIRE & COLLECTIONS
SA au capital de 182 938, 82 €
5, avenue de la République F-75541 Paris Cédex 11
Tel.: + 33 1 40 21 18 20
Fax + 33 1 47 00 51 11
www.histoireetcollections.fr

This book has been designed, typed, laid-out and processed by *Histoire & Collections*, fully on integrated computer equipment

Printed by ELKAR
Spain, European Union
December 2008